What people are saying:

"As president of our networking group, Peter taught many of his tricks of the networking trade. His enthusiasm for the subject is contagious, and his determination to make better networkers of us paid off in <u>higher volume of leads generated</u> for the group as a whole. In his view, every single point of contact is a networking opportunity."

Ellen R.—Past networking group president,
long time networking group member, business owner

"Peter has mentored me for over a year with his networking solutions and during that time I have been able to form a sales program that had <u>doubled my closed sales ratio</u>. If you want to increase sales, get a better job, or just learn how to know the right people, I highly recommend that you read this book and implement his strategies today!"

Steve K.—Sales representative

"Peter's ideas have increased my ability to make contacts and increase sales. By following his lead, I have been able to <u>open doors that I had thought closed before</u>. His enthusiasm, humor, personality, and character define "networking expert"."

Russ D.—Business owner

"Your contacts and book suggestions have already begun to help! I'm gaining experience & I'm making contacts."

Dave S.—Sales representative

More Leads

More Leads

The Complete Handbook for Tips Groups, Leads Groups and Networking Groups

Peter Biadasz

iUniverse, Inc.
New York Lincoln Shanghai

More Leads
The Complete Handbook for Tips Groups,
Leads Groups and Networking Groups

iUniverse books may be ordered through booksellers or by contacting:

iUniverse
2021 Pine Lake Road, Suite 100
Lincoln, NE 68512
www.iuniverse.com
1-800-Authors (1-800-288-4677)

ISBN-13: 978-0-595-36395-7 (pbk)
ISBN-13: 978-0-595-80830-4 (ebk)
ISBN-10: 0-595-36395-4 (pbk)
ISBN-10: 0-595-80830-1 (ebk)

Printed in the United States of America

Why Read This Book?

Would you like to shout?
I am in a networking group!!!
The leads will come to me like I am a lead magnet!!!

In my many years of working with networking groups, I have found that people get frustrated with their networking group because they either do not get enough leads from their networking group or they feel bad because they don't give many leads to their networking group members. This usually happens for one of two reasons:

They don't know how to give and receive leads.

OR

They don't *want* to know how to give and receive leads.

If you want to become a lead magnet, then read this book. It will be the best *work* that you have ever done in your life as a net*worker*.

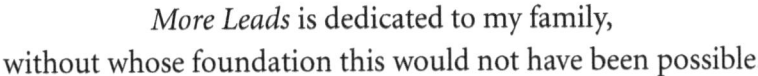

More Leads is dedicated to my family,
without whose foundation this would not have been possible.

Acknowledgements

I thank God for the abilities that I have been given; my wife and children for support and helping me learn more about myself than I ever thought possible; my parents who taught me through example many facets of networking and business; Zeedie, who not only saw potential in me but knew how to get that potential out of me; Terry—who invited me to my first networking group meeting; George and Jeff who hung in there with me in the early days of my networking group "career"; the T.B.L. Networking Group who let me experiment on them mercilessly; the local chamber of commerce who has supported me by allowing me to be more than just a volunteer in birthing, growing and participating in networking programs; the many networking groups and supporters that not only listened to what I had to say about networking groups but actually took the principles and applied them for the betterment of themselves as well as those around them; and Stephanie for some editing work. You all made an impact on my life greater that I can describe. Thank you all!!! Now your influence will impact those that read this book. Isn't networking great?

Contents

Preface

Do people actually read the preface in books? If you are one that does you get the *bonus advice.*

If you are a president of a networking group, then use the information in this book, never mention my name, and your group will think that you are a networking group genius. If you are a networking group member, read this book and give a copy of this book to your president to make him or her look like a networking group genius. Either way, you are well on your way to receiving many more leads from your networking group.

Introduction

What Is A Networking Group?

A networking group, leads group, tips group, etc. is an organization whose purpose is to assist in finding business leads for its members **and is your marketing department**. Each group usually has in it only one member of each represented industry, thus ensuring that there is no competition or professional category conflict within the group. Groups meet weekly, bi-weekly or monthly, depending on the goals of the group. Meetings are usually held at the lunch hour, although there are breakfast and evening groups.

You Need This Book If...

- ❑ You are **not receiving enough leads** from your networking group.

- ❑ You are in a networking group that is ready to **achieve the next level** in giving more leads.

- ❑ You are **not yet in a networking group** but want to see what the networking group world is all about.

How This Book Is Organized

More Leads will give you all the information you need to get many more leads from our networking group. The book is divided into several distinct sections.

Chapter 1 deals with the format of powerful networking group meetings and how to ensure that you are getting (and giving) the most in every segment of the meeting.

Chapter 2 gives you practical tips on what to do *before*, *during* and *after* any networking meeting that you go to. This will not only help you to enjoy the meetings more, but you will also see your lead getting (and giving) increase, which means that our income goes up.

Chapter 3 shows you the influence that you have as a networker to affect everyone that you know, and even those you don't know, in a very powerful way.

Chapter 4 gives you all the information you need to organize your own individual network of people. A network of organized networkers is unstoppable in today's business world.

Chapter 5 talks about leadership skills in networking groups and how leaders can be groomed to help make your networking group more powerful.

Chapter 6 tells you how to find a networking group if you are not in a group or are contemplating changing groups.

Chapter 7 gives you all the information that you need to start your own networking group.

Chapter 8 introduces you to the wider world of networking and how to take networking and your networking group to levels that you have never imagined and beyond.

Chapter 9 reinforces how you can base your business success on your networking group.

Chapter 10 evaluates your strengths and weaknesses as a networker, a networking group member and the strength and weaknesses of your networking group.

Chapter 11 presents a daily plan for networking success.

Chapter 12 ensures that you are performing at your fullest ability and potential.

Finally, the **Appendixes** will help assist in the exchanging of new ideas for the next several years in your networking group. **NOTE: If you have paid for this book and <u>are not being paid</u> to present the material from this book,** you have my permission to copy each handout *in its entirety* to pass it along to your group.

How to Use This Book

More Leads is a handbook, not a manual. It is a guide for you to use in developing your networking group to its fullest potential and a tool for you to use to become the best networker that you can be. As a handbook many of the ideas presented are open to your interpretation and can be molded to fit your particular situation. A manual would give inflexible detail denying you the option of molding this material to fit your circumstances.

Utilize the ideas in this book to energize your networking group meetings. *More Leads* gives you all the tools you need to have very powerful weekly networking group meetings for years to come.

Incorporate the teachings in this book as ways to operate your networking group. Take time each meeting to teach and discuss the ideas in this book with the membership.

At the end of every chapter there are challenges for you. As you complete each challenge, you will find that not only are you getting **more leads** from your networking group, but you are also becoming a very proficient and professional networker.

More Leads is a complete handbook for networking groups, leads groups and tips groups in that it brings to light the topics necessary to have the best group in your location as well as assist you in becoming a networker that is working at your fullest ability and potential. *More Leads* is not fully comprehensive in that volumes have been written about some of the individual topics covered in these pages. Utilize *More Leads* to understand which areas covered in this volume require further investigation or research for you to reach your desired goals. Then, and only then, will you find yourself giving and receiving more leads than you ever have in your professional career.

Peter Biadasz—a "Networking Expert?"

During the past 15 plus years I have been introduced to many groups and individuals by various titles, most commonly "the Networking Expert." This is a title that I have earned by not only being the most knowledgeable and proficient networker possible but also a passionate communicator, teacher and mentor to thousands of people, both in and out of networking groups, regarding the techniques and benefits of the networking of people in business and personal situations. I have been teaching networking by speaking to networking groups, company sales teams, writing articles on networking and related topics and in countless one-on-one mentoring sessions. Earning a college degree in psychology has helped in understanding and teaching the dynamics of interpersonal relationships. Utilizing common sense, performing much research and hard work has resulted in consistent sales success utilizing networking and my networking group as my main marketing mediums. Earning "Salesman of the Month" my first month in sales set the tone for my entire sales career. As a sales manager, I guarantee that my sales staff is #1 as they utilize their networks for win-win results. As a business owner, I have no doubt in success as networking continues to be the basis for my marketing efforts. Maybe a more appropriate title is "knowledgeable, passionate networker that is great at teaching networking". I am committed to the success of every networker that takes networking seriously.

CHAPTER 1

Meeting Format:
The Most Powerful Hour Of Your Work Week

Do you want to have a networking group meeting that is the highlight of everyone's week? If so, then you are in the right chapter. The following guidelines will show you how to have a networking group meeting that everyone will want to attend every time.

Starting The Meeting: Easier Said Than Done

You may think that starting a meeting is the easiest thing to do in this world. You stand, you call the meeting to order and everyone gives you his or her undivided attention. In the real world when it is time to start the meeting, people are walking in late, finishing their conversations, wrestling with their food order or one of many other distractions.

The first rule of the meeting is to start on time, every time. Let the group understand that this is their most important business meeting of the week and that they should be as prompt and courteous to the networking group meeting as they would any other sales appointment. They can finish their conversations after the meeting. It is always preferable to make arrangements with the meeting place regarding food so as to not interrupt the meeting. Teach by example to ignore distractions as the business of the networking group is the most important business of the moment

Welcome: Let's Get On The Same Page

No matter what time of the day or night that your group meets, always assume that everyone walking into the meeting has many things on their minds and needs to be put into a networking group frame of mind. The easiest way to do this, after a friendly welcome, is to read the group's purpose statement. Some groups also recite the pledge of allegiance. Whatever you do, it helps the group members set aside all the issues and troubles that they walked into the room with. After all, this meeting is supposed to be the highlight of their day, week, month, etc...

30-Second Commercials: Your Time To Shine

Your 30-second commercial in its weakest form will tell your group who you are, what company you are with, what you do and what a good lead is for you. At its best, your 30-second commercial is the most valuable teaching time that you have in front of your marketing department each week.

Think for a moment of the best TV commercial that you have ever watched, the best radio commercial that you have ever heard and the most memorable billboard that you have seen. Also, do you know how much money companies paid for a 30-second commercial in the last super bowl? Millions of $$$$$!!!

What Is Your 30-Second Commercial Worth?
How Memorable Is Your 30-Second Commercial?

These are the references that you should use for your 30-second commercial. This is your time to shine. Make it fun. Make it memorable.

The worst thing that you can do is stand up and say "Hi, my name is_____ and I work for _____." Not only is that not memorable but after hearing that introduction 15 times the group may be not so attentive, it may be asleep.

What is the marketing "hook" that your industry uses to gain customers? Use that "hook" in your commercial.

Remember, part of what you are doing during your 30-second commercial is training your marketing department—your networking group—how to find leads for you. In that process you should be as specific as possible as to what a good lead for you consists of.

There are two types of networking that the members can utilize to find those leads for you: *active* networking and *passive* networking.

In *active* networking, teach your group the questions that they can *ask* those that they come in contact with to find business for you. These are the same questions that you ask daily (qualifying questions) to get business for yourself.

In *passive* networking, teach your group what to look for and listen for to find leads for you. The best example of passive networking was a sign business in one of my networking groups that asked us to look for ugly signs. The town was full of ugly signs and he made it easy for us. All we had to do was provide the locations, not even a contact name. He received more leads each week than he could work. What a problem to have! In the copier business, reps asked group members to listen for the presence of copier techs in businesses that they may be visiting and even better yet, people that they heard swearing at their copy machines. *Passive* networking is fun and easy.

Do not be afraid to be different. I have heard people sing their commercial, rap their commercial, seen others stand on chairs during their commercial (be careful) and use all types of visuals that we all have in our industries. There have been many times I have utilized my trumpet during my 30-second commercial. Not only does it ensure that you have everyone's attention, it makes a memorable impression.

Then There Was "The Meeting"

Several years ago I was working with a networking group on improving every aspect of their meeting. After much teaching on how to give an effective 30-second commercial, the insurance agent in the group topped everyone and enhanced the marketing of his business tremendously. On a beautiful sunny day, in a crowded upscale restaurant he opened up a large golf umbrella to talk about his "umbrella" insurance policies, lit a fire to talk about fire insurance, then threw ice out of his water glass at us to talk about hail insurance. **He did all of this in 30-seconds.** The effects of which are still talked about today. He now owns his own insurance agency and has shown the value of giving great 30-second commercial.

Be creative. Do not be bashful. Your networking group is a safe environment to experiment as to how you present your business. Make a commercial that will be talked about for years to come. It will make your presentations outside of your group better than they have ever been.

Bonus: I have been using an extra topic to be inserted into the 30-second commercials each week to better learn about the people in the group. A list of topics appears in Appendix III, page 61, and I challenge you to utilize these topics to spice up the 30-second commercials of your group.

In closing, practice your 30-second commercial. A worksheet to assist you in making a memorable 30-second commercial is in Appendix II, page 59. You have known all week that you will be giving a 30-second commercial, do it like the professional that you are.

The Featured Speaker(s)

Usually one or two members of the group will give a 10 or 20-minute presentation that explains in greater detail all that their company has to offer. There are many great places to obtain information to become a more effective public speaker, but let me offer a few insights as to what makes an effective networking group presentation.

1. **Always give a 45-second history of your life from birth to the present.** The reason for this is very simple, as networkers we are constantly looking for ways to connect people. You will be surprised how many people in your networking group may know others that are from a town that is in your past, share the same educational institution that you went to, or may have worked at a company the you had worked at. This lets the group members get to better know you.

2. **Use visuals in your presentation.** Each industry has brochures, even if you make them for your group the morning of your presentation. However, be careful as to when you hand out your materials. After all, you want the group listening to you, not just reading while you are talking.

3. **Get your audience involved.** Ask questions of the group as you give your presentation. Better yet, let them know that you will be asking them questions at the end of your presentation and with prizes awarded. Bring small prizes like golf balls, promotional give a ways or better yet—cash.

4. **Take a moment and think about the best speakers you have ever heard.** You will quickly find that they all had one thing in common; they all knew how

to *tell a good story*. People love stories. But, each story must have a purpose in your presentation. We all have sales "war stories". Some are funny, some are sad but all will help keep your audiences attention.

5. The best way to know that you have a powerful and organized presentation is to **practice** it once or twice before the meeting. You will find that the presentation will be more enjoyable for you to give once you have worked the bugs out of it, it will be better received by the group, and that you will give better presentations to your prospects now that you are a polished presenter.

Do You Have A Fear Of Public Speaking?

Let me share with you how I overcame my fear of public speaking. For many years, I spoke in front of groups absolutely hating the speaking experience. But, I knew that to achieve my long-term professional goals I would have to give speeches. I disliked the experience so much that often I would get physically ill before making a presentation. For years, I used the sound of silverware hitting a water glass, *ding—ding—ding*, at the start of a meeting to calm me down like Pavlov's Dogs. Then I would button my suit coat and mutter under my breath "show time." On came the "happy face" and the audience never knew that I was terrified. After sharing this with a group (who did not believe me by the way), I found myself in front of the same group the following week. This time they heard me weakly say "show time" and realized I was very afraid of them, even though I was looked upon as their expert and leader. From that point on I share this: "if I can do it, you can do it" experience. Over time, I have actually learned to love public speaking. Yes, I still get the jitters from time to time. That is why I practice my speeches so much. But I do know that if I can make the long journey from getting sick before a speech to loving public speaking, then you can too.

Sharing Of Leads

This can be one of the best and worst parts of the meeting. It's great when the group members are passing a lot of leads to each other and reports of business being closed as a result are running rampant. But when there is so much silence in the room at this part of the meeting that you can hear hair grow, it's like death. So do your part, pass a lead every day to a member of your networking group. Later in this book I will discuss how easy it is to pass a lead a day. Finally, make it your goal to be the top lead producer in your group.

Lead Points

In Appendix IV, page 66, there is a sample form for group members to fill out weekly to award points for each part of the networking process. While the gaining of points is not supposed to be a contest, it can be if you want to have a little more fun. At its best, the points system gives more accountability of each member to the group, but more importantly it gives leadership an opportunity to see which group members are and are not involved in the networking process. I have found that networking group members usually do not get involved in the process of networking for one of two reasons, *they don't know how or they do not want to.* Most often the reason is the former rather than the latter. You see, most people join a networking group with no formal training in networking. The points system will show you which members may require some one-on-one mentoring or which topics can be shared in depth during the teaching part of your meeting. The points system is a great tool when used for the betterment of your networking group.

Based on the points sheet provide in the appendix, each member should have a minimum of 27 points per week, according to my networking priorities. While your priorities may differ, set the weekly goal for your group high but realistic. Then ensure that accountability is consistent. Finally, make it your goal to be the top point producer each week. *Lead by example!* You will be happily satisfied as to how the weekly points totals, i.e. the weekly networking group activity and everyone's business grows at a rate that will make your group the best it has ever been.

As for those that are not involved in the networking process because they do not want to be involved, they may want to seek a group that is not a "working networking group" instead of your group. (See Chapter 5—Handling Problems In Your Networking Group.)

Announcements And Group Business

Announcements are opportunities for the group to attend functions in the community, plan events for the group (see Appendix VIII, page 90, for a list of social events for networking groups) or notices to members of relevant information. Group business, usually the presenting individuals for membership or group financial reports, should be handled thoroughly yet swiftly. Nothing is worse than a meeting the gets bogged down and loses momentum. To ensure that these topics are handled smoothly, plan (usually with the other officers ahead of time) and practice the presentation, as you would any other professional presentation.

Teaching Time And Wrap-Up

This is my favorite part of the meeting, helping people become better networkers. Share with the group items out of this book or any other book, magazine or web site on the many topics related to sales, marketing, attitude, etc. Give handouts (see Appendix V, page 68, for sample handouts) so that the group knows that there is value in what is being shared.

You will find that the best way to know that you have learned something that you have read or heard is to share it with someone. Your networking group is a great place to realize that you know much more than you think.

Then challenge the group to set at least two appointments with group members before they leave the meeting (a great 30-second commercial topic would be to share how one of your one-on-one meetings went). How to have an effective one-on-one meeting is discussed in Chapter 2.

Finally, adjourn the meeting and let the group know that you hope that they have a great week.

This was the *Most Powerful* Hour of the Work Week!
(A sample meeting agenda is found in Appendix I, page 58)

Chapter 1 Challenge:
Decide **TODAY** that all of your networking group meetings will be the most powerful highlight of each member's week and implement the meeting guideline in this chapter.

CHAPTER 2

Before The Meeting, During The Meeting, After The Meeting: What Do I Do?

To get the most out of *any* networking meeting that you attend, there are a few simple things that you can do before, during and after the meeting that will ensure that you are using your time in the best fashion. And remember, every meeting that you have is a network meeting.

Before The Meeting:

Set Your Goals

Know in advance which people you want to talk to. By that, I mean not only which individuals that you know will be at the meeting but also which industries you may want to make contact with to fortify your network. In addition, make sure that you take the initiative and introduce yourself to all first timers at the meeting.

Prepare Your 30-Second Commercial

For details see Chapter 1 and Appendix II, page 59. You know in advance that you are going to present yourself, do it professionally and in a prepared fashion.

Prepare Questions To Ask The Speaker

When you know who the speaker is going to be, prepare one or two questions in advance to ask the speaker. This will not only help you to have a professional repoire but can aid in making good networking contacts.

Invite Guests

Many people want their networking group to grow but will not invite guests. Bring a guest, at least, every other week to your networking group meeting. It not only helps to enhance the group but also increases everyone's network.

Bring Business Cards And Other Written Materials

The exchange of business cards helps solidify a networking contact. There is no better way to ensure that you are getting peoples attention than to hand out written material while you discuss the material. However, do not just blindly hand out materials and cards. Make every contact count.

During The Meeting

Arrive On Time

Actually, arrive 15 minutes before the meeting start. This will give you an opportunity to meet with members that you have business with, greet visitors as they arrive, converse with the group leadership and get situated. If you know that you will be arriving late, let the president know in advance. That way your 30-second commercial may get presented, even though you are not yet present.

Be Alert

During every meeting, two things are going on at the same time: one person is speaking and everyone else is listening. The best way to be alert during networking group meeting is to take notes during the meeting. That way, if you think of a lead for someone during their 30-second commercial, you can immediately write it down rather that risk attempting to remember it for an hour during a meeting in which a lot of information is being presented.

Greet And Meet Visitors

Always take the initiative to greet and meet all visitors that attend your networking group. You never know what great things are waiting within that newly formed relationship.

Give A Memorable 30-Second Commercial

Your 30-second commercial is your time to shine. The section on this topic chapter in Chapter 1 and the worksheet in Appendix II, page 52, will aid you in making a memorable and powerful 30-second commercial.

Listen And Maintain Eye Contact With All Speakers

Let each speaker know through your eye contact that they have at least one person in the room that is interested in what they are saying. You will be amazed at how much more you will get out of your networking group by doing this: both in leads and in quality relationships. Also, whether you realize it or not, every time you listen intently to a speaker you are receiving a lesson in public speaking. Make note about what you like and dislike in the presentation to ensure that you incorporate the good and leave out the bad in your presentations.

Get More Brochures Of Your Group

If your group has a brochure, give it to everyone at the end of all your appointments. If you're group does not have a brochure, make one as soon as possible. This one marketing piece can improve the lead passing ability of you group overnight.

Example: at the end of an appointment, present the group brochure to your prospect, client, customer, family member, etc., and say "I belong to a group of professionals that meets every week. There are many industries in the group and based on what we have talked about it would be very positive for you to talk with (at this point you circle the names of the appropriate members on the brochure). When you call them, *use my name* and they will be happy to talk with you." Then when you can, call the group members whose names you circled and tell them who you left the brochure with. If they do not receive a call from that person in two or three days, the member should call them and *use your name* as a reference. You want everyone using your name. After all, *you are a networker, a total resource for everyone that you come in contact with.* By following this presentation after every appointment, you will pass at least a lead a day.

To realize the some of the potential that is unleashed with your networking group when everyone passes a lead a day look at the numbers: if every group member of a 15 member group passes one lead a day, that's 15 leads total a day or *75 leads a week* (15 leads x 5 work days) or *300 leads a month* (75 leads a week x 4 weeks) or *1,500 leads a year* (300 leads a week x 50 weeks, accounting for holiday time).

I am sure that you understand that if you are giving leads to your networking group members, you will receive your share of the 1,500 leads that may be passed within your group.

After The Meeting

Follow-Up As Appropriate

If you wrote down a lead for someone during the meeting, give him or her the lead immediately after the meeting. If you told someone that you would call him, make sure you call him. If you feel that you can add value to someone's situation, make sure you contact him or her. It may not be for business now but now is the time to start building a strong, sincere business relationship for future business consideration. You never know when that relationship will blossom into a prosperous business relationship.

Schedule One-On-One Meetings

Before heading for the car, take a moment and schedule one-on-one meetings for the upcoming week with at least two people from your networking group. When possible, meet at each others place of business. If that cannot be arranged, be sure that you meet in a place that is quiet and that no unwanted ears will be present to hear all of the vital and possible confidential information that you will share with each other.

Having an effective one-on-one networking meeting is very simple. Person "A" (you) asks person "B" (the person you are meeting with), "who or what is your target market?" While person "B" states who his or her target market is person "A" **writes down**, not trusting memory, everyone in the mentioned target markets that he or she knows. Having your network organized (see Chapter 4) greatly aids in this process. This lasts for 10-15 minutes. The written list is then given to person "B" with a check mark next to the people for which person "A's" name can be utilized in making the initial contact.

Then person "B" (the person you are meeting with) asks person "A" (you), "who or what is your target market?" While person "A" states who his or her target market, person "B" **writes down**, not trusting memory, everyone in the mentioned target markets that he or she knows. This also lasts for 10–15 minutes. The written list is then given to person "A" with a check mark next to the people for which person "B's" name can be utilized in making the initial contact.

Of course, the best case scenario is when both of you contact the individuals whose name you have written down to give an introduction for the other person. It is very important to give a public "thank you" in your weekly networking group meeting to the group members who exchange information with you. Also, let the information giver know when business has transpired thanks to their leads.

Catalog Information Gathered

Information is power! You will find that the information you gather weekly from your networking group has much power in it to share with your network at large. Keep track of all information that you receive so that it can be easily retrieved. You can do this via a hard copy filing system of electronically on a computer-based system.

Review Goals Set Before The Meeting

In order to evaluate if the meeting was truly successful, review the goals that you set out before the meeting to see whether or not you did all that you had expected. If not, get on the telephone and finish meeting your goals.

A, B, And C Groups

As your networking group grows you will find that it will be more difficult to pass leads and build solid relationships with everyone in the group. So to be more efficient, group each member into one of three groups. The "A" group will be your networking group foundation. Comprised of five group members, one for each day of the work week, these members are the members, because of similarity of industry or personality that you can and will give or receive the most leads from. Contact one member of your "A" group daily and you will be amazed what positive things will happen to your lead production and lead reception. You can actually have an "A" group meeting outside of your regular networking group meeting. You will be amazed at the higher amount of lead passing that can occur at an "A" group meeting.

Your "B" group are members that you will give and receive leads to on a semi-regular basis, again based on compatibility of industry and personality.

Finally, your "C" group members will rarely receive leads from you and you will rarely give them leads due to incompatibility of industries or personalities, but it is good to have them in your network at large. Also, it alleviates the guilt of not giving *everyone* in your group a lead. While it would be nice to give everyone leads, it may not be practical, especially in large networking groups.

No better example of this is when I was asked to consider allowing a funeral director into a group that I was president of. Talk about a possible uncomfortable situation. But, getting out of ones comfort zone is what networking is about. When you walk up to a group member you many times ask, "Is business going well?" You be uncomfortable asking a funeral director that question. Two weeks before the funeral director was to give his 20-minute presentation I told the group what the 30-second commercial topic was going to be so that they could prepare for it. The topic was to prepare their obituary. If they did not like what they saw as they wrote it, it was time for a course correction in their life. When it came time for the meeting, not only did we have 100 percent attendance, with everyone very prepared, but we also had requests from several non-members and presidents of other local networking groups to attend the meeting, with obituaries in hand. Not only did we have a truly life-changing meeting that week, we faced many of our fears, not your normal networking meeting. As for the funeral director, not only did he become an integral part of the group, he eventually served a year as president of the group doing an outstanding job. We also learned over time and through tragedy, the best time to get to know your funeral director, as with anyone in your network, is *before* you need them.

Lead Partners Or Lead Buddies...

As some groups call them, have been another tool to ensure that everyone in your networking group is really plugged into your group, especially as your group grows. Some groups assign lead partners every month. The partner process involves visiting your partner at their place of business or them visiting you at your place of business (see how to have a productive one-on-one meeting in this chapter.) In the case that one of you will miss the regular networking group meeting, you present each other's 30-second commercial just as good, or in many cases better, than if they were actually in attendance. Many great things can happen to group cohesiveness and lead productivity thanks to lead partner program.

Chapter 2:

Decide that from this moment forward that *before*, *during* and *after* every networking meeting, you will do all things necessary to give and get all that you can from each event.

Chapter 2 Goal:
Pass, *at least*, one lead per day, ***everyday*** to one person in your networking group.

CHAPTER 3

You Are A Networker:
A Total Resource For Everyone
That You Come In Contact With

Most people do not realize that they already are networkers and have been networkers all of their lives. The goal is to perfect the skills that are involved in becoming an effective networker. A matured polished networker works daily to create win/win situations for those that are in his or her network.

I have talked to people that have said that they have tried networking. They usually tell me that it worked for a while but it just faded over time. I tell them that *networking is something that you do, but being a networker is someone that you are.* And *by being a networker you are a total resource to everyone that you come in contact with.* While it is net**working,** not net**playing,** the transition from *networking* to being a *networker* is quite simple.

Successful networkers have many tools that they have developed over time. These include becoming extremely knowledgeable of their industry, as well as, the industries represented in their network, taking initiative in forming networking relationships, developing great listening skills, letting everyone know that they have quality contacts in a variety of industries that they would be glad to share, and creativity in connecting people and situations to meet obvious and hidden needs and wants.

Attitude: Your Most Important Asset

I have always felt that a person with a great attitude and mediocre competence would always be more successful than a person with a horrible attitude and good competence. Have you ever known someone with a bad attitude? When they called you or approached in public, didn't you find a creative way to avoid talking with them? What happens when you call someone? Can you picture them diving over a desk to get to the phone because *you* are calling them? Or are they intentionally sending the call to voice mail?

Would you be more likely to give a lead to someone with a good attitude or a bad attitude? If you are like me, you give leads to those people that will treat the customer the same way that you do.

Understanding that attitude is the most important asset that you have as a net-worker. Let me share with you some things I have done over the years to help maintain a positive attitude.

1. When the alarm clock makes that unpleasant sound in the morning, **make the decision** that you are going to be positive. Any decision made enough times becomes a habit. Being positive can be as much a habit as being neg-ative. When my alarm clock screams at me I just start praying. That usually helps my decision.

2. You can't put a smile on someone else's face unless you have a smile on yours so…**put a smile on someone's face by 9:00 a.m. everyday.** This can be the most fun for you and the most frustrating for those around you.

    I once had a boss that just hated it when I would pop my head in her office every morning to say a very cheery "good morning". However, two weeks after I left for a better position, I received a call from her letting me know that not only did she really appreciate the thought every morning but that her day was not the same because no one else was saying "good morning". You never know what kind of "seeds" you are planting.

3. You do not have to have the title of manager to be the **mood manager** of your company. Set the example and standard of what a positive attitude is at your place of business, at home and everywhere you go. You may be sur-prised how many people you can influence in this manner.

4. **Anticipate problems** before they happen. When was the last time a truly *new* problem presented itself, one that you had never been exposed too

directly or indirectly through your own or someone else's experience? Let's face it; so many times we get upset over the same thing. Time to develop a new habit (see 1 above)

5. Give **sincere compliments** on an hourly basis. Sincere is the key word. People will know if you are not being real in what you are expressing. Also, by complimenting others, you are looking for the good in them.

6. Finally, my favorite: **develop points of reference.** When you are going through a truly rough time, you can think in one of two directions: a) think about the best time of your life or something that makes you laugh as an escape or b) think about the worst time in your life and realize that you made it through that bad event so you can make it through this bad event.

Even though I am an optimist, I resort to thinking about two very bad events and realize that nothing I will go through will be as bad as these two events.

The first event occurred about a year after I graduated from college. While fixing breakfast one morning, I was holding a glass pitcher full of ice tea when all of a sudden the pitcher mysteriously just emptied itself. I put the pitcher down and took a step with my right leg, no problem. I then attempted to take a step with my left leg and it just didn't. Can't describe the feeling, or lack thereof, but when I looked at my left foot I saw an anatomy science project staring at me. I will spare you the gory details. (I save those for my public speaking engagements.) I knew I was in trouble and had to get to the phone in the next room quickly or I thought that I would be found in a slightly stiffened position that evening. The reality was that the bottom fell out of the glass pitcher and propelled by the weight of the liquid, turned in mid-air and cut my foot to the bone.

*Moral of the story: When faced with a bad situation I ask myself, "**Are all body parts attached?**" If the answer is yes, then what I am going through is not as bad as something from my past.*

The second event occurred a few years later as I worked in a bank branch. At closing time an armed, masked, body armored wearing person decided to rob our office. He knew about a large shipment of cash that we had received. The money was in a time locked vault that forced you to wait 10 minutes before you could access the cash. He decided to line us up in the vault stating that there were enough hostages to shoot some of us and still have people left to negotiate with to escape. I was number two in line. Feeling certain that the police would be there shortly, I had to resign myself that my life was about to violently end. Obviously there is more to the story as I live and breath today, but...

The moral of the story is: when faced with a bad situation involving another individual I ask myself, "Is this person literally holding a gun to my head?" The answer since the robbery has always been "no." So, no confrontation is as bad as the one from my past.

What Are Your Points Of Reference?

Sharing Your Network When They Call You

I will show you how to organize your network in the Chapter 4. The goal is for your network to realize that *as a networker you are a total resource for everyone that you come in contact with.* They know that if you do not know some one that can meet their needs, they know that you know someone that knows someone that can meet their need.

Examples: I once received a call from a realtor that had just sold a house to a family moving out of town that did not want to take their washer and dryer with them. So they called me to sell the washer and dryer. Now, I was not an appliance salesperson, but I did know of a realtor that had just sold a house to some first time homeowners that needed a washer and dryer. The set was sold in 20 minutes.

Another time a non-profit organization called me needing authentic Indian blankets. All I did was contact a Native American in my network and the organization had their blankets.

If your network is calling you for goods and services that have nothing to do with your real profession, you know that they will call you when they need your goods and services. It may end up being the easiest sale you have ever made. They trust you.

As a networker it is vital that you are successful in your chosen industry. People always like to deal with a winner. Always work to be the top producer in your company and industry. It always helps to be a student of your industry. If your network sees that you are a professional in your vocation, they will know that you a professional in the way that you network.

Networking Your Network When You Call Them

One of the funniest and most rewarding aspects of networking is networking your network. Basically, this is no more than introducing people that you know with each other. As the networking "matchmaker" (for business purposes, not romantic reasons), you can effectively match people based on common interests, compatibility of industries, or similar backgrounds. As a part of your introduction, remind the people being introduced to each other that the introduction is not only about them, but the meeting of two networks of people meeting each other.

Goal Planning

Thinking that you want to become a great networker is a good thing, writing down this goal along with a plan of action and a time frame to accomplish this goal turns the thought in your head from a dream or fantasy to something very real. You would not take a long trip without first looking at a map to see where you are going and which route is the best to get there. Our lives are a long journey; why not also map out that trip? No one wants a long trip to be boring and full of labors. We want our trips to be fun adventures that are rewarding. This is your life, your trip; make it the best that it can be.

There are many great goal-planning tools available to you. I have found the following process to be very useful when I am goal planning (a goal planning worksheet is located in Appendix X, page 93.)

1. List specific areas of your life that you want to evaluate. These areas can include: personal, professional, family, spiritual, financial, social, mental capabilities, personal development, personality traits, travel, education, material possessions, giving of time and/or money, skills, reputation, morals, emotional, physical, career, hobbies, fears, accomplishments, awards, mentors, reading, speaking, friends, values, time management, health, sleep, recreation, entertainment, transportation, living arrangements, self-esteem, your children, etc…Be thorough and examine every aspect of your life.

2. Make an *honest* evaluation of where you are right now in each area. Look at what you like and don't like about each area of your life.

3. In each area, list specific things that you would like to see as improvements, additions or deletions. Use your imagination and think outside of the box.

After all, it is your life. Why should you not live it to the fullest? The things listed in this area are your goals. Write down each goal.

4. Develop a written detailed plan to achieve each goal.

5. Prioritize each goal by time frame: one week, one month, one year, two years, etc…all the way up to 20 year goals.

6. Make a commitment to start achieving your goals today and show that commitment by writing down what you will do **today** to achieve each goal.

7. On a quarterly basis, review your goals. By doing this, you can feel good about your successes and progress while adjusting time tables on some goals as you move forward at a pace different than was originally planned.

8. Find others **that want to** achieve the goals that you want to achieve. Learn from them just as you can teach them how to achieve that goal.

9. Find others **that have already** achieved a goal that you may be working on. Not only can you learn new ways to achieve the goal but learn pitfalls to avoid in achieving the goal.

10. When you achieve a goal, reward yourself. It may be as simple as looking in the mirror and smiling at your self. Or in completing a larger goal, going on a cruise with someone. The bigger the achievement, the bigger the reward.

11. Feel good knowing that because you are planning and achieving your goals, every day, every week, every month, every year and every decade, your life can only get better and better.

You will find that the rewards of properly planning your goals greatly outweigh the work involved. Writing your goals makes them much more real to you.

During the months of December and January, I give many goal-planning workshops in networking groups. With the information in this section, have a goal planning session in your networking group. As the members of your group go through the goal planning process, you will be amazed at the improvement in your group, not just in the greater number of leads being passed, but at the increase in personal and professional success of the membership. Also, you will find that as your group members start achieving their goals, there will be more energy in your group and more leads will be passed.

Activity breeds activity! Success breeds success!

Procrastination

In my speaking presentations, I always take time to speak on the topic of procrastination. This is because it is so easy to be exposed to new ideas and then say to your self, "This is great stuff and I will start doing this next week". In reality, the time to start is now.

To overcome procrastination (use the procrastination worksheet found in Appendix XI, page 94)

1. Write down one thing that you have been putting off getting done.

2. Write down one thing that you will do between now and the time that you go to bed tonight to start getting this thing accomplished.

3. Write down how you will feel when you finally complete the thing that you have been putting off and finally…

4. Write down the name of someone that you will brag to that you finally got the thing done that you have procrastinated in doing.

In this process you have taken a negative and turned it into a positive. If it "was" a positive in the first place, you never would have procrastinated.

Over the years, procrastination has been a major hindrance to me. Here are some ideas that have helped me to overcome procrastination:

1. Think about why you procrastinate. As we go through life, there are many times we are required to get out of our comfort zones. Recognize your comfort zones and then expand those comfort zones.

2. Know what is important and what is not. Setting priorities helps in addressing the most crucial tasks in a timely fashion.

3. As you recognize what is important write them down. Thoughts when written, become reality.

4. When faced with large tasks, break them down into smaller, more manageable tasks.

5. Realize all the good that will happen as a result of finishing what you started, or just starting what you have been delaying. Good things always lead to more good things.

6. Be accountable and share your goals and ambitions with someone. As a result, you may find that doing an undesirable task with someone else will make it more rewarding. But don't always expect to recruit help when you share your goals.

7. Reward yourself after you have completed something that you have been procrastinating. However, do not intentionally procrastinate so that you can reward yourself.

8. Finally, do it and do it now!!!

Chapter 3 Challenge:

Decide that you will maintain a positive attitude and put the habit of procrastination in the past chapter of your life. The best way to show that you have done this is to write down your goals for the next week, month, year and two years. Write down one of these goals and an action plan to accompany the goal **before you go to bed tonight**.

CHAPTER 4

Your Network: You Know More People Than You Think You Know

We are all networkers, whether we realize it or not. Now that you realize that you are a networker, be the best networker that you can be. Not only do **you** have a network but everyone in your network also has a network. If you assume that everyone that you know knows 200 people (safe assumption based on how many people on average attend weddings and funerals,) and that you know 200 people, then your network represents 4000 people (200 x 200). **What would happen to your business if you received 4,000 leads today?**

Let's see the power of your networking group: if your network represents 4,000 people and there are 15 people in your networking group, and each of their networks represent 4,000 people, then each of your networking group meeting represent 60,000 people (15 people x 4,000 people represented by each member.) Do you see the power in your network? The fun really begins when everyone's network starts to network with each other's network. **What would happen to your business if you received 60,000 more leads?** That is how important your networking group is to you.

Who Is Your Network?

Your network is everyone in your professional and personal life from birth to the present time. You have a bigger sphere of influence than you think. You always have but it may have lost its power due to lack of organization.

Organizing Your Network

A few years ago, one of my mentors gave me a task that I thought was going to be more trouble that it was worth. I was so very wrong. The task was:

1. To take 90 days and write down the names of everyone that I had known from high school to the present. This meant going through yearbooks, address books, files, old letters and all sorts of information. (I am glad that I am a pack rat.)

2. The next task was to put them in alphabetical order. Today there are many types of software that can make this task easy.

3. I was then told me to start calling these people—all 750 of them. The format of the calls was quite easy; just find out what they were doing professionally. What their significant others were doing professionally and let them know what I was doing professionally. If all went well, I was told with just this activity I would never get beyond page one of my list because activity begets activity. That is just what happened. I got so busy with the leads that were generated from those call I never finished calling page one.

Organize you network in this manner and you are on your way to being the best networker you or anyone else has ever known.

Look At How Many Leads Are Under Your Nose

There is a tremendous difference between working smart and working hard. I have met so many "professionals" that were at a loss as to where they could find prospects or expand their network. Let's take a few moments and look closely at the people that are already in your family life, personal life and your professional life. As we do this, think beyond the obvious and discover that each person listed has a network of people just like you have a network of people. The long-term goal is to have members from each network meet each other.

People In Your Family Life

Fill in the blanks for the following areas of your family life:

Significant other   _____

Children   _____

Parents   _____

Brothers   _____

Sisters   _____

Grandparents   _____

Grandchildren   _____

Uncles   _____

Aunts   _____

Cousins   _____

Nieces   _____

Nephews   _____

In-laws   _____

Other family   _____

People And Places In Your Personal Life

Fill in the blanks for the following areas of your personal life:

Neighbors   _____

Neighbors' Place Of Employment   _____

Favorite Food Store   _____   Owner/Manager   _____

Favorite Restaurant:

    Breakfast   _____   Owner/Manager   _____

    Lunch   _____   Owner/Manager   _____

    Dinner   _____   Owner/Manager   _____

    Snack   _____   Owner/Manager   _____

Favorite Coffee House   _____   Owner/Manager   _____

Favorite Gas Station   _____   Owner/Manager   _____

Car Repair Shop   _____   Owner/Manager   _____

Oil Change   _____   Owner/Manager   _____

Favorite Organization   _____   Directors   _____

Favorite Charity   _____   Directors   _____

Your Hair Stylist   _____   Owner/Manager   _____

Your CPA   _____   Partners   _____

Your Financial Advisor _____

Your Banker   _____   Owner/Manager   _____

Your Lawyer   _____   Partners   _____

Your Cell Phone Vendor _____

Your Chiropractor   _____   Office Manager   _____

Your Doctor   _____   Office Manager   _____

Your Dentist   _____   Office Manager   _____

Your Realtor   _____   Owner/Manager   _____

Your Mortgage Banker   _____   Owner/Manager   _____

Your Dry Cleaner   _____   Owner/Manager   _____

Favorite Furniture Store_____   Owner/Manager   _____

Your Insurance Agents:

Life	_____	Owner/Manager	_____
Property and Casualty Agent	_____	Owner/Manager	_____
Your Travel Agent	_____	Owner/Manager	_____
Your Veterinarian	_____	Owner/Manager	_____
Your Church	_____	Church Board	_____
Favorite Club	_____	Owner/Manager	_____
Your Health Club/Gym	_____	Owner/Manager	_____
Favorite Clothing Store	_____	Owner/Manager	_____
Automobile Dealership	_____	Owner/Manager	_____

People Involved In Your Hobbies   _____

Other Places That You Spend Your Money: Look In Your Checkbook Register And Your Credit Card Statements

People And Places In Your Professional Life

Fill in the blanks for the following areas of your professional life:

Your Boss	_____	See Above Lists	_____
Your Co-Workers	_____	See Above Lists	_____
Your Customers	_____	Owner/Manager	_____
Your Suppliers	_____	Owner/Manager	_____
Financial Advisor	_____	Partners	_____
Banker	_____	Directors	_____
Company Lawyer	_____		
Coffee Service	_____	Owner/Manager	_____
Computer Specialist	_____		
Janitorial Service	_____	Owner/Manager	_____
Office Supplies	_____	Owner/Manager	_____
Promotional Products	_____	Owner/Manager	_____
Travel Agent	_____	Owner/Manager	_____
Advertising Vendors	_____	Owner/Manager	_____
Mentors	_____		
Landlord	_____		

Other Properties Owned By The Landlord _____

Other Tenants That You Landlord Has _____

		Owner/Manager	_____
Telephone Vendor	_____	Owner/Manager	_____
Water Vendor	_____	Owner/Manager	_____

Any other companies in the life of your company _____

Now that you have identified key areas of your family, personal and professional lives, **contact them all!!!** Learn about the network of people in their lives.

Adding To Your Network

Every contact you make every day of your life adds to your network. The goal is to keep your network organized so that when needs within your network arise, you can retrieve the network contact needed at a moments notice.

There are several sources of new networking contacts that we see daily but usually ignore. They almost always have current information regarding an existing company, including an address, telephone number, contact name as well as other important company or situation information. These sources include the many newspapers and magazines that come our way as well as the television and radio news advertising and public service announcements. I always read publications of any type twice, once for the articles and stories and the second time just to study the advertisers. After all, if they have the money to advertise, maybe they have the money to own your product or service.

The most overlooked source for expanding your network may be **your mailbox**. You will be amazed at how much your network, and your business, will grow if you call on the companies that send you what we may refer to as "junk mail". All of the current information that I mentioned in the previous paragraph, including company name, address, telephone number, contact name, etc…is delivered to your doorstep daily. I know many people that will pay a lot of money for prospect lists while at the same time ignoring key information that is given to them for free in their mailbox. The next time you look at your mail ask yourself "who in this stack should I contact for my benefit and/or their benefit." Maybe they are in your target market or better yet maybe they call **on** your target market. Why not pool resources? Your incoming mail is a stronger networking source than you realize.

You will also find that as your networking skills become more polished, your reputation as a networker, will result in **people seeking you out**. Everyone wants to network with and do business with others that are experts and strong sources of information, regardless of the industry. Your network will expand at times with little effort on your part due to the momentum that you have created in forming, organizing and nurturing your network. I receive many calls from people that I do not know, people that have heard about me from various sources, which want to network with me for the betterment of both of our business interests. Those meeting are the most fun and rewarding because not only is my network growing in an easy and unexpected way. But, often I find that we all know more people in common than you could ever think possible.

Remember, there is no such thing as an overnight success. Be patient, yet persistent, in your networking activities. You will find that over time you will build a network that will truly meet more needs than you ever realized possible. And as you become the ultimate resource for everyone in your network, you will definitely get more leads from you networking group.

Chapter 4 Challenge:
Over the next 90 days, take the time and organize your network in the manner described in this chapter.

CHAPTER 5

Leaders:
Every Group Wants One,
But Will *YOU* Be Our Next President?

Every organization will eventually take on the style of its leadership, whether it is a networking group or a country. In networking groups there are two levels of leadership, the formal elected leaders and the non-elected go-getters. Which one are you? Remember, you can have the title of an officer without being a leader and you can be a leader without the title of officer.

What Makes A Great Leader

Think about people in your life that have been great leaders in your eyes. While you can debate all day what makes a good leader, for networking groups I think it comes down to one very important attribute—**vision**. You can have every leadership quality from every leadership book but if you do not know where you are going, how can you get there and take the group with you? While you still need leadership qualities such as effective communication skills, organizational abilities, commitment, the ability to motivate others, emotional strength, focus, and ambition, a person with vision and the plan to carry out that vision will delegate to others in the group the areas that he or she is weak in to ensure that the vision is carried out.

This book contains my vision for an effective and productive working networking group. This vision has been proven; tried and modified over the years with many networking groups—both with me as the president, group member, consultant or speaker. Feel free to share this vision with your group and reap the rewards.

Supervision Versus Management Versus Leadership

Many people are elected as an officer of a networking group without realizing the distinction between supervision, management and leadership. While the three concepts and titles are closely related, they are distinctly different.

Supervision is comprised of two words, super and vision. As we discussed earlier, having vision for your group is very important. But to expand on this, your vision for your group must not only be superior, or super to the other group members, but you must be able to communicate your vision in such a manner that every member of your networking group sees your vision as if it were their own. In others words, everyone must have 20/20 vision when looking at your vision for your networking group.

Management involves the planning, organizing, leading and coordinating aspects of being a networking group officer. These are the behind the scenes activities that take place between the regular group meetings.

Leadership is the act of taking your vision that is super both in scope and communication and influencing the membership to not only follow the vision but actively fulfill the vision. In networking groups leadership by example seems to work the very best. Do you want more leads passed in the group? Then pass more leads yourself. Do you want your group to grow in members? Then brings guests to every meeting. Whatever you want from the group, achieve "it" by showing the group members how to do "it". Then encourage or require them to follow your example. When your vision is an extension of your commitment to the success of the group and its members, you will not have a problem having anyone follow your example.

By understanding these three very important concepts; supervision, management and leadership, you will be able to fully implement the steps necessary to be sure that your vision is super, understand how to implement the vision and finally lead your group to the completion of your vision for your group.

Becoming A Great Leader

There exists the age-old debate as to whether great leaders are born or made. Well, you were born, so let's make you a great leader. In becoming a great leader, we have already discussed the importance of having vision. At this point you are presented with the challenge of obtaining much information about leadership. There are basically four areas for you to concentrate on:

1. **Reading:** There is so much great information regarding leadership in books, magazines, on the internet, etc…Take time *daily* to read something on leadership. The best time of the day is the first 10 minutes of your work-day. Let me also make another strong suggestion, take a speed-reading class. Not only is this skill a great time management tool, but your reading comprehension will also improve. When I was in 10th grade, my parents forced me to take a night class with my dad (the joy of every 15 year old boy). The class was speed-reading. At the completion of the class, I read a several hundred-page book in 45 minutes that was assigned to me in my high school English class. I got an "A" on the book report, a first. I have been a supporter of speed-reading ever since.

2. **Listening:** Does your car have a tape player or CD player? Do you drive during the day, maybe to and from work or to appointments? You have a great opportunity to hear some of the greatest speakers and teaching in your car. Both bookstores and libraries have audio books, seminars, etc. available to you. Even fellow networkers may allow you to borrow their resources as you allow them to borrow yours. Some networking groups keep a formal list of resources that are within their group as well as a check out system similar to a library.

3. **Attending:** There are many seminars and workshops on topics that relate to your industry, sales, networking, leadership, etc. When you attend one of these events, sit towards the front, listen intently, take a lot of notes, talk with the presenter during the breaks, and network as much as you can (see *What To Do Before, During And After Any Networking Meeting* in Chapter 2 and *How To Get The Most From Any Networking Meeting That You Attend* in Appendix V, page 68.)

4. **Meeting mentors:** Do you know of some one that is already doing what you want to do? Then take the time to contact them and if possible meet with them. Most successful people will not only be flattered that you want to know about how they became successful but will share with you information that will be very valuable to you. In addition, there is a handout in Appendix XII, page 95, which shows you *How To Obtain Mentors*. Mentors can be instrumental in helping you in not only identifying both your strong and weak points but can assist in turning the weak points into strong points and the strong points into stronger points. You will be unstoppable!

In reading, listening, attending and meeting, do not only learn what people have done right to become successful and great leaders, learn from the mistakes that these people went through to become what they have become. Sometimes the "good old days" were also the "learning the hard way" days. Finally, to become a great leader of networking groups, make sure that you are doing everything that was discussed in Chapter 3. After all, how can you lead networkers, if you yourself are not the example to your group as to what a true networker looks, acts and smells like.

In Appendix IX, page 91, there is a list of 85 qualities that are attributes of a leader/networker. Study each quality using the four steps listed above: reading, listening, attending, and meeting to obtain the deeper meaning of each quality. In addition, during the teaching time at the end of each network group meeting, discuss one of the qualities each week. Not only will that give a group that meets weekly a teaching agenda for 85 weeks but it will teach every group member what it takes to be a leader, which is what a networker really is.

Networking Group Orientation Meetings

As the leader of your group, it is very important to know that every group member is aware of your agenda for the group. There is no better way to communicate that agenda than with an one-on-one meeting with each member. In Appendix XIV, page 99, is a meeting agenda to thoroughly orient each group member into your group. This will ensure that each group member, both veteran and new, will be fully aware of what is expected of them and that you have an open channel of communication as you fulfill your term in leadership. Topics included in the meeting are a review of the purpose of the group, an understanding of the by-laws, how the member can effectively market both themselves and the group members, lead passing expectations and the answering any questions that may arise. You will find that by conducting these networking group orientation meetings that many potential problems within your group can be addressed before they ever arise and that your group will reach their true networking potential much faster.

Handling Problems In Networking Groups

Every time I accept the presidency of a networking group my acceptance speech is always the same: I hold the groups by-laws over my head, thank the group for electing me president, throw the by-laws behind me as far as I can and the boldly proclaim that from now on there are only two rules: be on time and pass a lead a day, and if you stay with me I will teach you how to pass a lead a day.

Dramatic—yes!!! Effective—you bet!!! What I have done is laid down the law as well as my vision for the group. Every group that I have been president of has grown not only in numbers of leads but numbers of members. I have also set the criteria for handling problems within the group. When situations arise in a networking group, and trust me they will, there is only one question that the leadership of the group has to ask itself, *"What is in the best interest of the group?"*

If that question is at the forefront in solving any challenge facing the group, then the task of leadership is made that much easier. While each group does have by-laws to aid in the processes of the group, a strong leader will settle many things before they happen. Also, by setting the expectation of passing a lead a day and leading by example by passing at least a lead a day, when issues arise within the group leadership is dealing from a position of strength and example. I think that many problems arise in groups because the elected leaders are not in fact showing leadership.

Having stated the obvious, lets address some common challenges in networking groups:

1. **Not enough leads being passed:** After leadership has set the example in passing leads on a daily basis, utilize the points system to see who is not involved in the networking process and spend some one-on-one time tutoring them. Spend time teaching the group in the weekly meeting how to pass leads. Also, if need be, modify the by-laws so as to require a minimum number of point quarterly to maintain membership in the group. I know of one group that has a yearly retention vote of each member. While that is a strong procedure, it is a very strong group that passes a lot of leads.

2. **Members arriving at the meeting habitually late:** meet one-on-one with these members and remind them to treat this meeting as they would any other sales appointment. Habitual unexcused tardiness is a sign of disrespect and grounds for dismissal. After all, what is in the best interest of the group?

3. **Difficulty in getting members to volunteer to speak at the weekly meeting:** After showing the membership that speaking to the group will increase the number of leads that they receive from the group and after they have gotten over their fear of public speaking (see Chapter 1) you have one simple solution, you can volunteer speakers from the group if they do not volunteer themselves. I always have fun with this one: after asking the group who

wants to speak on specific dates, I volunteer the members that are straining to not have eye contact with me. Preference goes to new members or those veterans that have not spoken to the group in a while. I mentor the speakers on public speaking, usually one week before their presentation. You are after all, presenting the group members with an opportunity for growth.

4. **No one wants really wants to be the next president:** Networkers are leaders. As president, your job is to take your group to the next level, which includes leadership training, no matter how long it takes. I was president of on particular networking group for three and a half years. Much of that time was spent on leadership development and advanced networking techniques. The end result was amazing but not surprising. Amazing because I had never seen a networking group work at such a high level. Not surprising because of the professionals in the group.

   Note regarding by-laws: Even though the group's by-laws stated that a president could hold office for one-year terms, two terms maximum, the by-laws also stated that a by-law could be over-ridden with a two-thirds majority vote on the membership. Thus, I was president of that particular group longer than the prescribed time because they kept on voting me as president by more than the two-thirds required vote. In other words, if it isn't broke, don't fix it. Don't change leadership if all is going well just because the by-laws say so. Use your head with regards to common sense. The by-laws are a guide for the group. Know the by-laws and adjust the by-laws. Because the only question to be answered is: *"What is in the best interest of the networking group?"* (A sample of networking group by-laws is found in Appendix VI, page 83.)

5. **The group has no excitement:** That is **your** responsibility, *whether or not you are in leadership in the group.* Just as you do not have to have the title of manager to be the mood manager at work, you do not have to have the title of president to be the mood manager of your networking group. The best way by far to create excitement would be to pass leads and then pass more leads. After mentoring and teaching the group the networking group techniques in this book, ask the non-participants to leave the group. Make sure that each industry slot in your group is filled with an excited and productive networking professional. Do not settle for second best in any area.

6. **Attendance at the meetings is low:** If you have already implemented the remedies stated in 1–5, you can offer an incentive to the group for the weeks that there is 100 percent attendance. Ask the group what type of

incentive they want to see what motivates them. Check with the group treasurer to see what financial resources are available and with the group members to see what products and services may be donated to the group for the benefit of the group. A lunchtime group may use something as simple as the group paying for dessert for the lunch that day to celebrate 100 percent attendance. Be creative! What a win/win scenario!

If any other problem arises in your networking group, then I ask that you remember two simple guidelines: Ask **"what is in the best interest of the group?"** If you cannot answer that question then look at the group's by-laws.

Chapter 5 Challenge:
Decide today that you are gong to be the best leader that your networking group has ever had.

CHAPTER 6

Finding A Networking Group: All Dressed Up With No Place To Go

At this point you may be thinking one of four things:

1. "I am currently in a great networking group."

2. "The networking group I am in has potential and I am the one to move my group to the next level."

3. "My group is the most pathetic on this planet and it is time to find a new group."

4. "I am not in a networking group, but I want to be."

Points one and two are discussed throughout this book. Now, let's visit on points three and for, but not in that order.

Looking For A Networking Group

Finding a networking group is easy. Finding a great networking group may take a little work. Places to look for networking groups include:

- Lour local chamber of commerce
- Business section of your local newspaper
- Business or trade publications
- Yellow pages

- Asking top Sales people that you know

- Business owners

- Internet

After announcing to my customers that I was switching from my current career to outside sales, one of my customers invited me to visit his networking group. Upon accepting his invitation, I had only one question, "What is a networking group?" Having no idea that such organizations existed. I visited, joined, was president three months later, and have been "preaching the gospel of networking groups" ever since.

It is recommended that you visit two or three groups before you decide which group is for you. You want to join a group that you feel comfortable in. There should be a strong match between your personality and the personality of the group that you join. Look for members industries that you know will be good lead sources for you with the knowledge that you can pass solid leads to them. Examine the dues structure of the group. If the cost of membership is higher than the costs to cover the food, make sure that you are getting your money's worth.

As you contact each networking group president note the following items: meeting time (starting and ending), meeting location, *the time that most members arrive to network before the meeting*, the makeup of the group (if possible have someone fax you a roster of the group), meeting format, membership procedures and member expectations.

When you visit the group be sure that you bring a lot of business cards. Follow the steps previously discussed in Chapter 2 of what to do before, during and after the meeting to ensure the best evaluation of the group and to get the most out of the meeting. Even if you do not join that particular group, you have still made some potentially valuable networking contacts for the future.

Finally, find a group that passed a lot of leads. After all, the true purpose of the group is to pass leads.

Changing Networking Groups

I receive many calls from people saying that they are not receiving any leads from their networking group and they need help in finding another group.

The first thing I *think* is "is this person a follower or a leader?" So the first thing I *ask* is "how many leads a day or week do you give to your group members?" If the answer is a low number, or as usual, none, then I tell them the truth, "**the best way to get a lead is to give a lead.**" Then I tell them that they have a tremendous opportunity to be the lead giving leader of their group and talk to them about many of the networking group techniques mentioned in this book.

If after the conversation the person appears energized I will give them all of the long-term support that they need to make their group prosper. If over time, they have given their all to the group and the group did not respond in a positive fashion, then I gladly help them find a group that deserves them.

However, if after the conversation it appears that this person did not want to do the work required in effective networking: then I let them know that changing networking groups will not increase the amount of leads that they receive, only changing their networking habits. This is not exactly what they wanted to hear but sometimes the truth is brutal. Every now and then I receive a repeat call form these people stating that they are ready to lead, not just follow the apathetic crowd. Then the rewards begin!!!

Chapter 6 Challenge:
Take immediate action to make your networking group the best it can be.
If you are not in a networking group, visit three this week and join one next week.

CHAPTER 7

How To Start A Networking Group: When All Else Fails, Do It Your Way

Every networking group started with one person who could not find a networking group to belong to. It may have been that there were no openings in a group due to industry classification, no group that met that person's criteria or maybe there was not a networking group in the geographic area to join. Whatever the reason, starting a networking group is quite simple. Making it the best networking group ever is where the fun is.

Before Your First Meeting

In order to form a networking group:

1. Find a core group of 3-5 people in different industries that you know and trust who are committed to growing their business through a networking group. A list of industries is found in Appendix VII, page 88.

2. Decide if the group will meet at breakfast or at lunch (most groups are lunch groups.)

3. Choose a day and time for the group to meet. Choosing the right restaurant is very important. While quality networking, and not the food, is most important, an environment that is conducive to networking will add a lot to the group. This means meeting in a room that is not noisy so that all group members can hear each other and having the meal orders taken and food served in such a manner so as not to interrupt the flow of the meeting.

4. Set your agenda for the meeting and use the tools in this book to aid in making your networking group a powerful one. And even though it goes without saying, because you formed the group, congratulations, **YOU** are the first president.

Your First Meeting

Every meeting, whether it be two people or 50 people should be the same. Never apologize for the size of your group. All that matters is that everyone is passing leads and getting connected into each other's network. With that type of excitement and substance, visitors will want to join your group and the size of the group will take care of itself in a very positive way. (Use the meeting format detailed in Chapter 1 or condensed in Appendix I, page 58 and you can't go wrong.)

Now The Fun Really Begins

You have your own networking group. To keep it alive will be the hardest and most rewarding work you will have ever undertaken. Over time you will share in the rewards and growing pains that accompany any worthwhile undertaking. When times are going well for the group have the members share all the success that they can attribute to being in the group. When the group runs into challenges, have the members share all the success that they can attribute to being in the group. Your biggest challenge will be finding a group of committed networkers that will see the group through its stages of growth. At one point early in my networking career, I had a stretch of about four months with meetings of just two or three people (including me) in attendance at the weekly meeting. But the skills learned during that time aided me to preside for three and a half years over a group that reached 42 members. The destination is worth the journey.

Chapter 7 Challenge:
Find someone in your network that is looking for a networking group. If they cannot join your group, either help them find a networking group or help them start a networking group.

CHAPTER 8

The Networking Of Networks

Do you want your networking group to reach levels even greater that what we have talked about so far? Do you want to become the best networker on this planet? Then you are ready for the next level of networking group and net-worker maturity: networking your networking group with other networking groups—locally, nationally and internationally.

You Are Not Alone

I was involved in my first networking group for what seemed like an eternity before realizing that there were many other groups like mine. Some were more successful and some less successful than my group, but they were all "hungry" for ideas, motivation and just wanted to know that they were not alone in experiencing the normal problems that networking groups face. In fact, they wanted to know what the normal challenges were, and whether they were nor-mal or abnormal as a group.

The good news is—you are not alone.

However a word of caution, in networking networks rule one is "*Thou shalt not steal personnel from another group.*" It is healthy for groups to grow by having co-workers from other group members join their group. However, it is really frowned upon when members jump to another group because *the grass looks greener on the other side.* Keep integrity in your networking activities.

Networking Local Networks

These are the steps to organize a network of networking groups:

1. Identify the groups that are in your geographic area. This can be done through the local chamber of commerce, looking in the local business section of the newspaper for networking groups that advertise in the local events areas or by placing inquiries yourself in newspapers, magazines, etc.

2. After the groups have been identified, you can go in one of three directions:
   a. Plan a function that involves only the leadership of the networking groups.
   b. Plan a function that involves all of the networking group members.
   c. Plan a function that involves only the leadership of the networking groups to plan a function that involves all the members of the networking groups. In my opinion, option c is the best option.

In my town, option 2c is called the *Presidents Council* and I am very grateful to my local chamber of commerce for their support of our *Presidents Council*. One hour each month, local networking group presidents or their designate, usually another officer from their group, meet for one hour to:

1. Educate the networking groups and their leadership on how to increase the effectiveness of the groups and increase lead production amongst their members.

2. Be a forum in which the groups can have a meaningful exchange if ideas and information.

3. Discuss what is and what is not working in their groups. Each group may provide encouragement or present ideas to deal with challenges that groups face.

4. Discuss innovative things that they do in their networking groups to make their group the best group in the area.

5. Announce vacancies by industries that they are attempting to fill.

6. Receive topics for the weekly 30-second commercials.

7. Discuss relevant community topics such as upcoming events, new businesses, regulatory information, etc.

8. And most importantly, plan events that all of the networking group members can attend. For the past several years, our local *Presidents Council* has sponsored a chili cook-off in February or March, a dessert bake-off in June and an educational event in September. In preparation for the chili and dessert events, each group has there own mini contest at one of their own networking group functions with the winner advancing to the "city finals". At the chili cook-off, we also have a baked potato bar for the non-chili lovers. The dessert bake-off is held in a park or a facility that can hold the event. One of our local networking groups has within it a barbeque cooking company that caters the event with the best barbeque that I have ever had. The educational event is a luncheon. The speakers and topics are based on suggestion that the groups have filtered through the *Presidents Council*. The admission to the events is just enough to cover expenses and families are welcome to the some of the events depending on the logistics.

A list of social events for networking groups is found in Appendix VIII, page 90. I have always thought that city wide networking group talent show would be a lot of fun. We did a talent show in one of my networking groups a few years ago with great success.

The Bigger Picture

We have discussed networking on a local level but as you can guess there are networking groups throughout your state, country as well as internationally. While there are many sources to find other networking groups (chambers of commerce, business sections of publications, the internet, etc.,) I must shamelessly promote my web site, please visit **www.getmoreleads.net**. Not only can you post your networking group and make contact with other groups but you will be able to access a wealth of information on topics related to getting more leads from your networking group. Finally, you will have the opportunity to share your networking experiences, both good and bad, for the benefit of the networking community. It will be another tool available to you and your group to reach your fullest potential.

Chapter 8 Challenge:
Get plugged into the network of networking groups in your community. If no such network exists, start one.

CHAPTER 9

How To Make A Profitable Career Based Only On Your Networking Group (Your Marketing Department)

Hopefully by now, you are realizing the enormous business potential that is in your networking group. Each member has a network that, if shared with you, could result in a measurable increase in your business. So let's recap how to make sure that you are on your way to letting your networking group be the basis for you business success.

Training Your Marketing Department

Every week you have four vehicles available to properly and thoroughly train every member of you networking group:

1. Your prepared and memorable 30-second commercial

2. One-on-one meetings with at least two members of the group

3. Leads that you give to networking group members

4. Leads that you receive from networking group members.

In addition, you have the opportunity to give a full presentation to the networking group as a whole on occasion. If you are consistent and persistent in each of these areas, you will find that your networking group, **your marketing department,** is fully and properly trained.

Marketing Your Marketing Department

Everyday is filled with opportunities to market your marketing department. Get in the habit of including something about your networking group at the end of every sales presentation. This actually accomplishes two things: it markets your networking group daily and allows everyone that you come in contact with to see you as a networker—a person who is more valuable to them than just the product or service that you offer.

Also, does **everyone** in your network know about your networking group? Today, start marketing your networking group to everyone in your network. Visit them, call them, e-mail them, write them, it does not matter how you do it. What matters is that you are marketing your networking group to everyone in your network. Finally, you can register your networking group at getmore-leads.net for the whole world to see.

Obtaining Business From Your Marketing Department

Ask daily for leads, for referrals, for information. But do it only after you have given leads, referrals and information. The best way to get a lead is to give a lead. **Give daily!!!** Also, as you have contact with anyone in your network, either at events, on the telephone, e-mail or note, give them sincere words of encouragement regularly. You will find that you receive leads just because people like you.

Chapter 9 Challenge:

Ensure that your networking group is properly trained, that you market your group on a daily basis and that you give and receive a lead every time you talk with a networking group member.

CHAPTER 10

Evaluating Your Foundation As A Networker

How good a networker do you want to be? Do you want to be known as a total resource to everyone that you come in contact with? Or, do you want to be just like everyone else? Because you are reading this I think that you want to become the total resource to everyone that you come in contact with. As you may know, the bigger the building, the stronger the foundation must be. Let's discuss the areas that make your foundation as a networker. The end of this chapter and Appendix XIII, page 83 has an evaluation worksheet that you can use to grade yourself in each of the following areas:

Evaluating You

- **Goals:** Do you have comprehensive, clearly defined written goals with timelines? Is one of those goals to be known as a networker, a total resource for everyone that you come in contact with?

- **Attitude:** Is your attitude positive and improving?

- **Leadership Skills:** Have you identified and daily cultivating leadership skills through appropriate books, tapes, CDs, videos, seminars and mentors?

- **Your Network:** Is your network organized and growing daily?

- **Mentors:** Do you have mentors to aid in identifying and correcting your weaknesses while helping to fortify your strengths?

- **In a Networking Group:** Are you in a networking group?

Evaluating Your Networking Group Participation

- **Attitude:** Are you the example of positive attitude in you networking group?

- **Attendance:** Are you at every networking group meeting? If not, do you notify an officer in advance of your absence?

- **A Leader in Passing Leads:** Are you the top lead producer in your networking group?

- **Visiting Networking Group Members:** Have you visited **every** networking group member at their place of business? Have you had **every** networking group member visit your place of business? Do you have at least two one-on-one meetings with networking group members every week?

- **Memorable and Effective 30-Second Commercial:** Do you prepare in advance a commercial that your networking group considers to be the best commercial each week?

- **Marketing Your Networking Group:** Have you talked about your networking group and its members to each of your customers, prospects, family, friends and in every sales presentation?

Evaluating Your Networking Group

- **Goals:** Does your group have a clearly defined mission?

- **Organization:** Does the group have an organizational structure conducive to passing a high number of quality leads?

- **Attitude:** Is your network group meeting the highlight of your workweek?

- **Lead Passing:** Does the group pass leads daily?

- **Leadership:** Does the leadership have a vision for the group's future and has that vision been effectively communicated?

- **Potential:** What do you see as the long-term success of your networking group? Remember, anything that you do not like about your networking group, you can change for the better.

The Written Evaluation

On a scale of 1 to 10, with 1 being the worst and 10 being the absolute model of perfection, grade yourself in the following areas vital to being a true networking professional:

Evaluating You

Goals _____

Attitude _____

Leadership skills _____

Your network _____

Mentors _____

In a networking group _____

Total (Perfect score is 60) _____

Evaluating Your Networking Group Participation

Attitude _____

Attendance _____

A leader in passing leads _____

Visiting networking group members _____

Memorable and effective 30-second commercial _____

Marketing your networking group _____

Total (Perfect score is 60) _____

Evaluating Your Networking Group

Goals _____

Organization _____

Attitude _____

Lead passing _____

Leadership _____

Potential _____

Total (Perfect score is 60) _____

You may want to share this evaluation with members of your networking group. To do so, copy the handout in Appendix XIII, page 97.

Chapter 10 Challenge:
Become a "10" in each area evaluated in this chapter.

CHAPTER 11

The Week In The Life Of A Networker

The week of a networker is enjoyable, organized and productive. Everyday is a new adventure. When you get out of bed in the morning you do not know who you will add to your network, whose network you will be added to or how these events will occur. While the day-to-day routine may seem routine, the journey is not. And that is when business happens!!!

Monday:

- ❏ Family Time
- ❏ Attitude Check
- ❏ Growth Time
  (Read, Educational Tape Or Video, Mentor, Etc…)
- ❏ Review Network Database
- ❏ Add To Network Database
- ❏ Call Two Networking Group Members
- ❏ Visit One Networking Group Member
- ❏ Plan Memorable 30-Second Commercial
- ❏ Sign new business
- ❏ Ask For Referrals
- ❏ Give A Lead
- ❏ Receive A Lead
- ❏ Research Your Network
- ❏ Attend Appointments
- ❏ Ask For The Business
- ❏ Market Your Networking Group
- ❏ Plan Tomorrows Activities
- ❏ Attend Network Group Meeting If On This Day.

(All of Monday's activities are covered in this book. Review as needed.)

Tuesday:

❑ See Monday

Wednesday:

❑ See Tuesday

Thursday:

❑ See Wednesday

Friday:

❑ See Thursday

Saturday:

❑ Family time

❑ Be aware of your surroundings and the people in them as you have never been before

❑ Document your findings

Sunday:

❑ See Saturday

❑ Rest

Chapter 11 Challenge:
Live the life of an effective networker every day.

CHAPTER 12

You Are The Center Of Your Networking Universe

You now have all the information you need to not only have an incredibly powerful networking group but also to be a very successful networker. After evaluating your foundation as a networker do you begin the process of improvement by improving you, your network or your networking group? The answer is "yes" to all the above. You may decide which area is the weakest and place the greater emphasis there, but by working on each area daily you will find much satisfaction in the results of your marketing efforts.

Each network meeting should be the highlight of your week. Remember, you do not have the title of president to be presidential in your networking group. While you need to respect the chain of command, if you feel that your group is not working up to its full potential, then become that top lead producer in the group and attempt to add as much to each meeting that you can. *You are the mood manager of your networking group.*

Organization is a very important tool to networkers. You now know everything you should do before you go to each meeting, how to get the most out of every meeting that you go too, and the important steps to follow after each meeting. Perform each step as if you success depends on it. In fact, your success does depend on it.

You have a much larger network that you could ever imagine. Your network makes you a very powerful person. By organizing your network, adding to it daily and contributing leads to those in your network, your power as a networker grows daily.

Networkers are leaders, or at least, leaders in training. You have at your finger-tips all that you need to reach the next level of leadership that is within your capability. The acquisition and refining of leadership skills is a lifelong process. Aren't you glad you have the time? I am happy that we also discussed how to overcome procrastination.

Whether you are in a networking group, looking for a networking group or starting a networking group, realize the marketing potential at your fingertips. You networking group truly is your marketing department, just as you are a part of your network's marketing department. Everyday is a new and exciting experience as you see how the different parts of your network interact with you and each other to achieve mutual success.

The result is simple and exciting: MORE LEADS!!!!

Chapter 12 Challenge:
Review the challenges from chapters 1 thru 11 weekly and ensure that you are completing each challenge to the very best of your ability and potential.

Appendixes

APPENDIX I

Sample Meeting Agenda And Format

Start The Meeting	2 Minutes
Welcome Of Members And Visitors	2 Minutes
Introduction Of 30-Second Topic	1 Minute
30-Second Commercials	15-20 Minutes
Featured Speaker(S)	20 Minutes
Announcements And Group Business	8 Minutes
Teaching Time And Wrap-Up	7 Minutes
Total Time	**60 Minutes**

One Power Packed Hour

From the book *More Leads* by Peter Biadasz

APPENDIX II

30-Second Commercial Worksheet

Key points of information:

- ❏ Who you are? _____
- ❏ What do you do? _____
- ❏ Your is your company name? _____
- ❏ What a good lead is for you? _____
- ❏ Active networking:

  What are the qualifying questions you ask to get business?

  _____

  _____

- ❏ Passive networking:

  What should the group members look for and/or listen for to find good leads for you?

  _____

  _____

- ❏ What visuals can you use? _____
- ❏ What is a memorable opening statement? _____
- ❏ What is your memorable presentation style? _____

Now that you have the elements of your presentation, you need to decide which order they will be presented. Write your 30-second commercial and then *practice, practice, practice.* Your 30-second commercial is key in training your marketing department to get more leads for you.

Appendix III

30-Second Commercial Topics For Meetings

To be used to enhance the 30-second commercials and learn more about your group members

Business Topics

1. Complete the sentence: "If I were president of this group, the first thing I would do is…"

   (All presidents should use this topic at least once and write down how the group finishes the sentence. You then have your agenda for your term as president.)

2. Who is your favorite customer (and why aren't they in your networking group?)

3. Perform the 30-second commercial for the person to your right/left, or pick a member's business card out of a hat. (How can you get a lead for someone unless you know who he or she are, what he or she do and what is a good lead for him or her?)

4. Why are you in this networking group?

5. What quality do you admire most in leaders?

6. What is the best book that you have ever read?

7. What or who is your favorite source of leads?

8. What part of your job do you like the most?

9. Name one of your accomplishments from the past week.

10. What is the industry that you most like to work with?

11. What is the best lead that you have ever received?

12. What is your favorite quote?

13. Define success.

14. Name some of the organizations that you belong to.

15. Who is your main competitor?

16. Define character.

17. Name a company that you have had trouble securing business with. (Someone in the group may know someone there.)

18. Name one thing that you have done in the past week to improve yourself.

19. What awards have you won in your career?

20. What are your favorite business related websites?

21. Where is the best place to buy business clothing?

22. What other networking events do you attend?

23. Who has been your best mentor?

24. How are you going to exceed your goals this year?

25. What is the most effective marketing that you have experienced?

26. What is thing that sets you apart from your competitors?

27. What is your secret to successful time management?

28. If you could interview one person in history, who would it be and why?

29. What is your ideal lead for you?

30. Tell us about your latest one-on-one meeting with a group member.

31. When are your busiest and slowest times of the year?

32. How do you let you customers know that you appreciate them?

33. What motivates you?

34. What is the biggest lesson you have learned from any of your mistakes? (Those that can walk on water are exempt from answering.)

35. Besides your networking group, where else do you network?

36. If you could add one more industry to the group what would it be?

37. Who is the best boss that you have ever had?

38. If your professional life were a movie (song or book,) what would its title be?

39. Why are you an asset to this networking group?

40. What is the favorite product that your company offers?

41. What is your major accomplishment for this year?

42. How do you prepare for the weekly networking group meeting?

43. How do you handle sales objections?

44. How do you get customer referrals?

45. On a scale of 1 to 10, with 10 being perfect, rate yourself as a networker. What can you do to improve your networking success?

46. How have you used e-mail to improve your business?

47. What is one thing that you want people in your group to tell prospects about you?

48. How do you prepare for a sales appointment?

49. Create a topic based on today's meeting speaker.

50. Create a topic based on current events or time of year.

Personal Topics

1. What are your hobbies? (You may find that group members, customers and prospects may share the same interests, and common interests are one basis for networking.)
2. What is your strongest (weakest) quality?
3. What is your favorite social activity?
4. Name your favorite vacation location?
5. Name one of your greatest fears.
6. What career did you want when you were in high school?
7. Who was the teacher that influenced you the most?
8. Name one of your talents.
9. How many siblings do you have and what are their ages?
10. What makes you happy?
11. What is your favorite dessert?
12. What is your most prized material possession?
13. Where is the best place to go for dinner?
14. What was you all-time favorite class in school?
15. What is your all-time favorite movie?
16. What is the best financial advice that you have ever received?
17. What was your most embarrassing moment?
18. If money were no object, how would you spoil yourself?
19. What is one thing that you want to do before the end of the year?
20. If your personal life were a movie (song or book,) what would its title be?
21. What is one thing that you wish everyone knew about you?
22. What are the occupations of your family (parents, siblings, spouse, offspring, etc.)?
23. Where is a great place to go for a weekend day trip?
24. Tell us about your pets past or present.
25. What is the nicest thing about you?
26. What is your ideal house?
27. What was the best day of your life?

28. Where do you see yourself five years from now?
29. What is your favorite time of the year and why?
30. Create a topic based on what you know about your group members or maybe you want you know about your group members.

Appendix IV

Networking Group Activity Points Sheet

Purpose: To enhance your awareness, on a daily basis, of the activities that lead to the success of the members of our networking group

Activity	Value	Earned	Notes
Qualified Referral	5		
Referral	3		
Lead	1		
Gave a group brochure or directed someone to group web site	1		
Attended Weekly Meeting	1		
Initial purchase from a member	3		
Met with a member	2		
Transacted business resulting from a member's lead	5		
Lead given resulting in business	10		
Made presentation to group or provided a speaker	10		
Sponsored new member	1 month free dues*		

After the new member's third month anniversary.

Lead: General information with no mention of the networking group members name.

Qualified referral: Introduced the name and business of both the networking group member and the prospect to each other.

Referral: Give the networking group member permission to call on a person and/or business using your name.

From the book *More Leads* by Peter Biadasz

APPENDIX V

Handouts For Your Group

People always seem to perceive that a meeting has more value when they leave with something in their hand. Always make sure that the teaching time at the end of your meetings includes a handout.

Following are some handouts that I have found to be very effective over the years. Some very successful people use these handouts as wallpaper in their offices as a reminder of what it takes to be successful. In addition, quotes that have motivated or instructed you make great handouts. Present them in the same manner as the quotes on the following pages.

> **If you have paid for this book and <u>are not being paid</u> to present the material in this book,** you have my permission to copy each handout *in its entirety* to pass it along to your group.

"The best way to get a lead is to give a lead!"

Peter Biadasz
Networking Expert

From the book *More Leads* by Peter Biadasz

My goal as a networker
is to
pass at least
one lead
<u>everyday</u>
to one person
in my network.

From the book *More Leads* by Peter Biadasz

How To Get The Most From Every Networking Meeting You Attend

Before The Meeting

1. Set your goals
2. Prepare your 30-second commercial
3. Prepare questions to ask the speaker
4. Invite guests
5. Bring business cards and others written materials

During The Meeting

1. Arrive on time
2. Be alert
3. Greet and meet visitors
4. Give a memorable 30-second commercial
5. Listen and maintain eye contact with all speakers
6. Get more brochures of your group

After The Meeting

1. Follow-up as appropriate
2. Schedule one-on-one meetings
3. Catalog information gathered
4. Review goals set before the meeting
5. A, B and C groups

Please keep in mind that the more you put into the meeting,
the more you will get out of the meeting!!!

From the book *More Leads* by Peter Biadasz

Who received a lead from me today?

From the book *More Leads* by Peter Biadasz

EVERYTHING

is an opportunity for <u>someone</u>
in your networking group!

From the book *More Leads* by Peter Biadasz

"**Networking** is something that you do.

A **Networker** is someone that you are."

Peter Biadasz
Networking Expert

From the book *More Leads* by Peter Biadasz

By being a networker you are a <u>total</u> resource for <u>everyone</u> that you come in contact with.

From the book *More Leads* by Peter Biadasz

What is the best use of my time RIGHT NOW?

From the book *More Leads* by Peter Biadasz

The Habit Of Networking

Networking

From the book *More Leads* by Peter Biadasz

Networking is not about *you*, it's not about *me*, it's about <u>US</u>.

From the book *More Leads* by Peter Biadasz

Networkers build bridges, not walls

From the book *More Leads* by Peter Biadasz

The more organized *your* network, the greater *your effectiveness* as a networker.

From the book *More Leads* by Peter Biadasz

You do not have to have the title of *manager* to be the *Mood Manager* of your office!

From the book *More Leads* by Peter Biadasz

The best day to network is *every* day that ends in "Y"

Peter Biadasz
Networking Expert

From the book *More Leads* by Peter Biadasz

APPENDIX VI

Sample Networking Group By-Laws

By-Laws of *Networking Group* Name

ARTICLE 1

Networking Group Name

The name of this association shall be *Networking Group Name.*

ARTICLE II

PURPOSE

The purpose of this association is to benefit members by referring business to one another. It is understood that networking is an integral part of any business. Members will also exchange ideas and information, which may benefit other members. Members are encouraged to do business with other members; however, there is no requirement that they do so.

ARTICLE III

MEMBERSHIP

1. Any person of good character, good business or professional reputation, may be eligible for membership. Each member shall be classified in accordance with his/her business or profession. The membership shall consist of only one from each classification of business or profession. Membership is

owned by the individual member and not by the company represented; membership cannot be transferred or assigned.

2. Membership in another organization with similar objectives constitutes a conflict of interest and is prohibited.

3. Membership in *Networking Group Name* shall automatically terminate if and when a member ceases to be personally and actively involved within the geographic area in his/her business or professional classification, or severs his/her connection with his/her business establishment, or resigns from the association. Any member who is absent from two (2) consecutive regularly scheduled meetings of the association (**unexcused,**) or misses 50 percent or more of the meetings in any quarter, and has not requested a leave of absence, will be expelled.

4. Any member may have an excused absence by notifying an officer, or his/her lead partner **prior** to the meeting, or by notifying the Secretary within 24 hours after the missed meeting of the reason for being absent.

5. When the membership of a person has terminated as provided in Article III, Section 4, such person may reapply for membership according to the stipulations of the By-laws.

ARTICLE IV

ADMISSION OF NEW MEMBERS

1. Any member may propose a candidate for membership in accordance with membership provision in Article III.

2. A prospective member shall be invited by any *Networking Group Name* member to attend a regular meeting as a guest and will be asked by the Secretary to complete a membership application. During the meeting, he/she will be asked to make a brief presentation to the membership concerning his/her business and to respond to inquiries from the membership. The applicant's signing of the application shall constitute his/her agreement to abide by the By-laws of *Networking Group Name*. If no objections to the prospective member are made, a vote on his/her membership will be taken at the next regular meeting of the association. The prospect should not be present during the vote. A unanimous vote of approval of the membership is necessary for acceptance into the association. The President will contact the applicant: concerning approval/denial of the application.

ARTICLE V
OFFICERS

1. The association's officers shall be: President, Vice President, Secretary, Treasurer, and Assistant Treasurer, along with the Immediate Past President, these officers constitute the Board of Directors.

2. The term of office shall be twelve (12) months, from January through December.

3. A member shall serve no more than one (1) consecutive term in the same office, unless a unanimous vote of membership agrees to reelect an officer in the same office.

4. During the first regular meeting in November members of the group will make nominations for each office. The nominations are to be publicized and posted by the Secretary in the remaining November meetings.

5. During the third regular meeting of November each individual that has accepted a nomination will speak to the group and address the following points:
   a. Why seeking the office desired?
   b. Plan/Goal for the office during term.

6. Elections will be held the first regular meeting in December. Ballots will be tabulated and reported to the group at the end of the same meeting by the current Secretary and Treasurer.

ARTICLE VI
DUTIES OF OFFICERS

The President has overall responsibility for the direction of *Networking Group Name.* The President shall preside at the weekly meetings and generally guide the affairs of the association. He/She shall be responsible for welcoming each new member to the club by letter. The President shall form committees for whatever purposes or projects deemed necessary and shall appoint Chairmen for each committee.

The Vice President shall serve in the President's absence. The Vice President is responsible for all programs.

The Secretary keeps attendance records and is responsible for the reparation of current membership.

The Treasurer collects monthly dues and properly accounts for them. He/She will pay all bills in a timely fashion, and at the first meeting of each month, will make a financial report to the members.

The Assistant Treasurer will assist the Treasurer in all aspects of the Treasurer's duties.

ARTICLE VII

MEETINGS

1. The association shall meet weekly at a time and place selected by the membership. A change in the time and/or place may be made by a majority vote of the membership.

2. A quorum is defined as one-half (1/2) of the membership.

ARTICLE VIII

DUES

1. Dues shall be set by the membership and may be changed from time to time as necessary by a 2/3 vote of the membership.

2. Dues shall be payable no later than the first regular meeting of each month and shall include the cost of lunch.

3. If a member's dues become one (1) month in arrears, the Treasurer will report the delinquency to the membership in the monthly financial report. Two (2) consecutive month's arrearages shall be grounds for termination of membership in the association.

4. New members shall pay first and last months dues at initiation of membership.

5. A current member shall receive one (1) month free dues when the following criteria is met:

   a. The current member Sponsors/Introduces new members for membership in *Networking Group Name.*

b. Upon new member being accepted for membership, he/she pays dues as agreed in Article VIII, Section 4.

c. New member is active for ninety (90) days and is current on dues.

ARTICLE IX
TERMINATION OF MEMBERSHIP

1. If any member engages in conduct demeaning the professional image of *Networking Group Name,* his/her membership may be terminated by a majority vote of the Board of Directors.

2. When the points system of tracking networking activity is being utilized, any member that has less than 300 points per quarter may be terminated by a majority vote of the group membership.

ARTICLE X
AMENDING BY-LAWS

To amend the By-laws the following must occur:

1. Member shall propose in writing, during a regular meeting, any changes desired.

2. Proposed amendments shall be distributed in writing to each member during the next business meeting for discussion. Any changes to the proposed amendment will be corrected and submitted for a vote during the following business meeting.

3. A 2/3 majority of the membership must agree to amend such By-laws.

From the book *More Leads* by Peter Biadasz

APPENDIX VII

Industries That Are Common To Networking Groups

Following is a list of 56 industries that would be of benefit in your networking group.

- ❑ Awards
- ❑ Banker
- ❑ Beauty Consultant
- ❑ C.P.A.
- ❑ Carpet Cleaning
- ❑ Cell Phone
- ❑ Chamber of Commerce
- ❑ Chiropractor
- ❑ Coffee Service
- ❑ Commercial Real Estate
- ❑ Computer Network
- ❑ Computer Repair
- ❑ Photography
- ❑ Credit Card System
- ❑ Dentist
- ❑ Dry Cleaning
- ❑ Insect Exterminator
- ❑ Financial Planner
- ❑ Florist

- ❑ Funeral Service
- ❑ Furniture
- ❑ Hair Stylist
- ❑ Heating and A/C
- ❑ Hotel/Motel
- ❑ Insurance—Life
- ❑ Insurance—Property & Casualty
- ❑ Interior Design
- ❑ Janitorial Service
- ❑ Landscaping
- ❑ Lawyer
- ❑ Local/Long Distance Dial Tone
- ❑ Mailing Equipment
- ❑ Massage Therapist
- ❑ Mortgage Banker
- ❑ Mover
- ❑ Office Supplies
- ❑ On-Hold Messaging
- ❑ Paint & Body Shop

- ❏ Payroll
- ❏ Photographer
- ❏ Plumber
- ❏ Printer/Copy Shop
- ❏ Professional Sports Teams
- ❏ Promotional Products
- ❏ Radio
- ❏ Realtor
- ❏ Security Systems
- ❏ Signs
- ❏ Staffing—Temporary
- ❏ Staffing—Permanent
- ❏ Telephone Systems
- ❏ Television
- ❏ Travel Agent
- ❏ Uniform Service
- ❏ Veterinarian
- ❏ **Your** Industry

Other Industries:

_____

_____

_____

_____

APPENDIX VIII

Social Events For Networking Groups

Here is a list of social activities that your group can use to get to know each other, and if you want, each others families and friends, in a relaxed and fun manner

"A" Group Luncheon	Golf Outing
Attend Sporting Events	Holiday Parties
Bake Sale	Horseback Riding
Bowling	Laser Tag
Bungee Jumping	Makeup Party
Camping	Museum
Canoeing	Open House at Member's Business
Car Races	Paintball
Chili Dinner	Parachuting
Concert	Picnic
Cookout	Playing Pool
Dance	Political Gathering
Dance	Pool Party
Dessert Bake Off	Religious Gathering
Educational Opportunities	Sail Boating
Field Trip	Swimming
Fishing	Talent Show
Game Night	Trade Show
Garage Sale	Volleyball

From the book *More Leads* by Peter Biadasz

APPENDIX IX

Positive Qualities Of A
Leader/Networker

On the following page is a list of 85 positive qualities that are attributes of a leader/networker. Study each quality, using the four steps listed in Chapter 5 regarding leadership: reading, listening, attending and meeting, to obtain the deeper meaning of each quality. Then during the teaching time at the end of each network group meeting, discuss one of the qualities each week. Not only will that give a group that meets weekly a teaching agenda for 85 weeks, but it will teach every group member what it takes to be a leader, which after all, is what a networker really is.

Positive Qualities Of A Leader/Networker

(See Guidelines On Previous Page)

Action Oriented
Ambitious
Assertive
Authoritative
Balanced
Bold
Caring
Character
Committed
Communicator
Competent
Confident
Considerate
Consistent
Conviction
Courageous
Creative
Decisive
Dependable
Disciplined
Empathetic
Encourager
Energetic
Energized
Energizing
Enthusiastic
Expectant
Fair

Faithful
Family-Oriented
Flexible
Focused
Forgiving
Goal-Oriented
Grateful
Greeter
Happy
Hard-Working
Healthy
Honest
Honorable
Hopeful
Humble
Humorous
Initiator
Integrity
Intelligent
Knowledgeable
Listener
Loyal
Motivated
Open-Minded
Optimistic
Organized
Passionate
Patient

Persistent
Personable
Planner
Positive
Positive Attitude
Powerful
Practiced
Prepared
Pride
Punctual
Quality
Refreshing
Resourceful
Responsible
Secure
Self-Esteem
Sense of Humor
Sensitive
Sincere
Student
Talent
Teacher
Team Player
Tough
Unselfish
Values
Visionary
Winner
Wise

From the book *More Leads* by Peter Biadasz

Appendix X

Goal Planning Worksheet

Area to be addressed: _____

Current situation: _____

Desired situation: _____

Specific goal to be achieved: _____

Action plan: _____

Time frame: _____

My reward when the goal is achieved: _____

From the book *More Leads* by Peter Biadasz

Appendix XI

Procrastination Worksheet

What am I procrastinating?

_____
_____
_____

What is one thing I will do before I go to bed **tonight** to start completing the item I listed:

_____
_____

When I get this completed, I am going to reward myself by:

_____
_____

From the book *More Leads* by Peter Biadasz

Appendix XII

Mentor Exercise

Name Three Of Your *Strongest* Qualities:

1. _____ - _____
2. _____ - _____
3. _____ - _____

Next to each quality, name someone that shares that same quality as his or her strong point.

Name Three Of Your *Weakest* Qualities:

1. _____ - _____
2. _____ - _____
3. _____ - _____

Next your weak quality, name someone that possess that quality as a strength.

Assignment: Meet with at least one of the people listed above for each of the next six weeks (a different person each week) to discuss the qualities listed and learn how they were are able to excel in these areas.

Reminder: "Turn **weak** qualities into **strong** qualities and **strong** qualities into **stronger** qualities."—Peter Biadasz, Networking Expert

APPENDIX XIII

Your Networking Report Card

On a scale of 1 to 10, with 1 being the worst and 10 being the absolute model of perfection, grade yourself in the following areas vital to being a true networking professional:

Evaluating You

Goals _____

Attitude _____

Leadership skills _____

Your network _____

Mentors _____

In a networking group _____

    Total (Perfect score is 60) _____

Evaluating Your Networking Group Participation

Attitude _____

Attendance _____

A leader in passing leads _____

Visiting networking group members _____

Memorable and effective 30-second commercial _____

Marketing your networking group _____

    Total (Perfect score is 60) _____

Evaluating Your Networking Group

Goals   _____

Organization   _____

Attitude   _____

Lead passing   _____

Leadership   _____

Potential   _____

    Total (Perfect score is 60)   _____

APPENDIX XIV

Networking Group Orientation

Topics to include:

- Review of group purpose

- By-laws, especially dues and attendance requirements

- 30-second commercial "How To's"   Page 9

- Lead passing expectations   One Daily

- One-on-one meeting "How To's"   Page 16

- Review of group brochure to identify A, B, C group members Page 17

- Networking theory & how to look for and pass leads   Page 10

- Answer any questions

"The best way to get a lead is to give a lead"

Peter Biadasz
Networking Expert

From the book *More Leads* by Peter Biadasz

Index

About the Author

Peter Biadasz (pronounced *bee-ahd-ish*) has been working with networking groups since 1989 in various capacities including president, consultant, speaker as well as a very active member. Peter has been a networker all of his life. A graduate of Florida State University, Peter's passion for and expertise in the areas of networking groups and the networking of people has aided many people in getting more leads form their networking group. In addition, the groups that Peter works with experience an increase in the quality and quantity of leads passed, an increase in the number of group members and an excitement for networking as never before as group members transform into quality maturing networkers.

For more information, please visit www.getmoreleads.net.

978-0-595-36395-7
0-595-36395-4